THREE BILLBOARDS
OUTSIDE EBBING, MISSOURI

THREE BILLBOARDS
OUTSIDE EBBING, MISSOURI

Martin McDonagh

ff

FABER & FABER

First published in 2017
by Faber & Faber Limited
Bloomsbury House
74–77 Great Russell Street
London WC1B 3DA

Typeset by Country Setting, Kingsdown, Kent CT14 8ES
Printed and bound in the UK by CPI Group (UK) Ltd, Croydon CR0 4YY

A CIP record for this book is available from the British Library

ISBN 978-0-571-34529-8

2 4 6 8 10 9 7 5 3 1

MAIN CAST AND CREW

FOX SEARCHLIGHT PICTURES AND FILM4

present

A BLUEPRINT PICTURES PRODUCTION

A MARTIN MCDONAGH FILM

MILDRED	Frances McDormand
WILLOUGHBY	Woody Harrelson
DIXON	Sam Rockwell
ANNE	Abbie Cornish
ROBBIE	Lucas Hedges
DESK SERGEANT	Željko Ivanek
RED WELBY	Caleb Landry Jones
ABERCROMBIE	Clarke Peters
PENELOPE	Samara Weaving

with

John Hawkes as CHARLIE

and

Peter Dinklage as JAMES

Written and Directed by	Martin McDonagh
Produced by	Graham Broadbent
	Pete Czernin
	Martin McDonagh
Executive Producers	Bergen Swanson
	Diarmuid McKeown
	Rose Garnett
	David Kosse
	Daniel Battsek
Director of Photography	Ben Davis, BSC
Production Designer	Inbal Weinberg
Film Editor	Jon Gregory, ACE
Costume Designer	Melissa Toth
Music by	Carter Burwell
Co-Producer	Ben Knight
Casting by	Sarah Halley Finn, CSA

Three Billboards
Outside Ebbing, Missouri

EXT. BILLBOARD ROAD — DAY

Mildred Hayes, a woman in her early fifties, driving along a country road, passes an old billboard, roadside. Whatever advert was on it is long since faded and torn. Mildred drives on, to a second billboard a few hundred feet along the road.

She notices this one a little more, though its old adverts are equally ramshackle. She slows to a stop.

After looking up at the billboard a while, she slowly reverses and stops at the first, then looks at all three, stretching away to the quiet horizon.

Makes a mental note of EBBING BILLBOARD ADVERTISING, *then drives on again, leaving the three old billboards alone like tombstones on the dusty road.*

INT. WELBY'S OFFICE, EBBING ADVERTISING — DAY

Red Welby's office, window looking on to Main Street and the town's police station. Red, a cool-looking young guy, pretends to read a Penguin Classic as he observes the office hottie, Pamela, pass in a cute dress. Mildred strides on in.

> MILDRED

You Red Welby?

> RED

Yes, ma'am. How may I . . . ?

> MILDRED

They said those three billboards out on Drinkwater Road, you're in charge of renting them out, that right?

> RED

I didn't know we *had* any billboards out on . . . Where *is* Drinkwater Road?

3

MILDRED

Road out past the Sizemore turn-off no one uses since the highway got put in.

Red checks a file. Mildred observes a beetle on its back on the windowsill, trying to right itself.

RED

You're right. Got three billboards out there. Nobody's put nothing up out there since . . . 1986. That was 'Huggies'.

MILDRED

How much to rent out all three of 'em the year?

RED

The year? You wanna pay for three billboards on a road no one goes down unless they got lost or they're retards, for a year?

MILDRED

Quick, ain't ya, Welby?

RED

Well . . . since what I say goes these days down at the Ebbing Advertising Desk, I'm gonna strike you a real good deal on those billboards, now, what was it you said your name was, Mrs . . .?

MILDRED

What's the law on what ya can and can't say on a billboard? I assume it's ya can't say nothing defamatory, and ya can't say, 'fuck', 'piss' or 'cunt'. That right?

RED
(*taken aback*)

Or . . . 'anus'.

MILDRED

Well, I think I'll be alright then. Here's five thousand for the first month. I assume that'll cover it.

She plonks down five thousand dollars cash.

And here's what the billboards oughta say.

She hands him three index cards, then moves to the window. He reads the first, the second, the third. Stunned.

> MILDRED
>
> Why don't ya draw up a little contract betwixt us while you're at it, make sure no one rents them billboards out from under me?

Welby looks up at her sadly.

> RED
>
> I guess you're Angela Hayes' mother.

> MILDRED
>
> That's right, I'm Angela Hayes' mother.

Mildred, at window, gently sets the beetle back upright. It waddles off happily. Behind it, the US flag flutters above the police station, as a couple of laughing cops enter it.

> MILDRED
>
> Name's Mildred. How long before you've got 'em put up?

> RED
>
> (*checking calendar*)
>
> Oh, shall we say by . . . Easter Sunday?

Mildred stares out at the police station.

> MILDRED
>
> That'd be perfect.

EXT. COP CAR DRIVING ON BILLBOARD ROAD — NIGHT

Officer Dixon, thirty-five, drives up the billboard road and approaches, from behind, the third billboard. Two Latino workmen work on it, buckets and squeegees. As he passes he looks up at the posters on it, double-takes, screeches to a halt.

The billboard reads, in large, stark letters HOW COME, CHIEF WILLOUGHBY?

> DIXON
>
> Hey! What the hell's this?!

                              LATINO

Que?

                              DIXON
'How come, Chief Willoughby?' what?

                              LATINO

What?

                              DIXON

Yeah!

                              LATINO

Huh?

                              DIXON

How come what?

                              LATINO

What?!

                              DIXON
Listen, I better start getting some straight answers outta
you Mexican sons of bitches . . .

*The second Latino has pointed to the distant second billboard, making
an odd little gesture, and Dixon looks over . . .*

*Dixon's point-of-view: the back of the second billboard, and the black
guy finishing up with the posters there. End point-of-view.*

Dixon sighs, drives off towards it.

EXT. BILLBOARD ROAD, SECOND BILLBOARD — CONTINUOUS

Dixon swings his car around to the front of the billboard. It reads AND
STILL NO ARRESTS? *The black guy, Jerome, is emptying out his
buckets.*

                              DIXON
                          (*to himself*)
What the Hell is this? (*To Jerome.*) Hey you? What the fuck
is this?

                                6

JEROME

What the fuck is what?

DIXON

This! This!

Jerome turns around and reads, as if for the first time.

JEROME

Advertising, I guess.

DIXON

Advertising what?

Jerome reads it again.

JEROME

Something obscure?

DIXON

I'll say!

JEROME

Don't I know your face from some place?

DIXON

I dunno, do ya?

JEROME

Yeah. Yeah, I do.

Jerome spits on the ground, looks at him with disdain. Dixon stares back; a vicious edge between them.

DIXON

I could arrest you right now, if I wanted to.

JEROME

For what?

DIXON

For . . . emptying out your bucket there. It's against the . . . being-bad-against-the-environment laws.

JEROME

Well, before you do that, Officer Dixon, why don't you go

have yourself a look at that first billboard over there, and *then* we can have ourself a talk about the motherfucking environment. How about that?

Dixon looks at the distant first billboard, standing all alone, back to us, the dark sky behind it. Dixon sighs, starts his car, pulls away.

We go with him, staying on his face, as he comes to the first billboard and slowly stops in front of it. His face falls.

DIXON

Fuck me.

He takes out his cellphone, and presses 'Willoughby (home)'.

INT. WILLOUGHBY HOUSE — CONTINUOUS

Chief of Police Bill Willoughby, fifty, having dinner with his young wife, Anne, mid-thirties, and his two daughters, Polly, five, and Jane, seven. The telephone rings.

ANNE

Don't, William . . .

Willoughby, sheepish, answers it.

WILLOUGHBY

Dixon, you goddam asshole, I'm in the middle of my goddam Easter dinner . . .

EXT. BILLBOARD ROAD, THIRD BILLBOARD — CONTINUOUS

Dixon is out of the car now, pacing.

DIXON

I know, Chief, and I'm sorry for calling ya at home and all, but uh, I think we've got kind of a problem . . .

As Dixon passes out of frame, the first billboard is revealed. It reads RAPED WHILE DYING.

Wide shot of the three billboards stretching away to the distance.

EXT. BILLBOARD ROAD — DAY

Mildred drives Robbie, her seventeen-year-old son, past the billboards – checking his reaction. He sees them but gives nothing away.

EXT. SCHOOL — DAY

She drops him at school. He heads off without a goodbye.

EXT. MAIN STREET — DAY

She drives up Main Street. Sees activity outside the police station – Willoughby with his Desk Sergeant, forcibly telling Dixon to stay behind, then crossing street to Red's place.

EXT. GIFT SHOP — DAY

She continues to the other end of town, a gift shop she works at. Mildred's co-worker, Denise, black, twenty-eight, smokes outside.

                    MILDRED
          Sorry I'm late, Denise.

                    DENISE
          Did you put up those billboards to fuck with the cops yet?

                    MILDRED
          They're up.

                    DENISE
          You go, girl! You go fuck those cops up!

She pats Mildred on the back, tosses her cigarette away, and they go inside.

INT. WELBY'S OFFICE — DAY

Quick-fire dialogue, Red at desk, Desk Sergeant and Willoughby standing.

                    DESK SERGEANT
          What the fuck do you think you're doing, Welby? Buncha

billboards like that, you didn't think there'd be some kinda *ramifications*? *Legally?*

                    RED
What's the legal ramifications, Cedric?

                DESK SERGEANT
You want me to explain the legal ramifications, a little punk like you? And don't call me Cedric.

                    RED
Ain't contravening no laws on *propriety*, ain't contravening no laws on any fucking thing. I checked all this up.

                DESK SERGEANT
Oh yeah, where'd you check all this up?

                    RED
In a . . . book.

                DESK SERGEANT
Which book, genius?

                    RED
Book called 'Suck my ass, it's none o' your business'.

Willoughby gives him a long cold stare.

                 WILLOUGHBY
How long has this person, or persons, rented these billboards out for?

                    RED
Oh, the year.

                 WILLOUGHBY
And how long she actually *paid* for?

                    RED
The year.

                 WILLOUGHBY
So it's a 'she', is it?

                    RED
                 (*pause*)
Ain't at liberty to divulge that kinda information, Chief.

WILLOUGHBY

Mildred Hayes, perhaps?

RED

Ain't at liberty to divulge that kinda information, Chief.

WILLOUGHBY

Do you really wanna fuck with the Ebbing Police Department, Red? Do ya?

RED

I guess.

INT. POLICE STATION, WILLOUGHBY'S OFFICE — DAY

Willoughby, Desk Sergeant and Dixon.

DIXON

He said what?! To your face?!

DESK SERGEANT

No crime has been committed here.

DIXON

Defamation of character ain't a crime?

DESK SERGEANT

It isn't defamation if she's simply asking a question.

DIXON

What are you, an idiot?

DESK SERGEANT

Don't call me an idiot, Dixon.

DIXON

I *didn't* call you an idiot. I asked if you *was* an idiot. It was a *question*.

WILLOUGHBY
(*smiling*)

He got ya there, Cedric!

DIXON

Well, I'm gonna do something about it if yous two ain't.

> WILLOUGHBY

Where you going? Don't fly off the handle!

But Dixon has already stormed out.

> DESK SERGEANT

Why in hell you keep that man on, Bill?

> WILLOUGHBY

He's a good man. At heart.

> DESK SERGEANT

He tortured a guy in custody, Bill.

> WILLOUGHBY

There was no . . . real evidence to support that.

As Welby is coming out of his building, Dixon crosses the road towards him.

> DIXON

Take 'em down.

> RED

Hah?

> DIXON

Take 'em down.

> RED

Take what down?

> DIXON

You think I wouldn't take you out, right here on Main Street, Red?

> RED

Thought you only take out black dudes, Dixon . . .

Dixon goes to punch him, but Willoughby is suddenly there, grabs his punching arm and shoves him towards the station. People on the street are staring, especially the blacks.

> DIXON
> *(to Welby)*

Ain't nobody never goes down that road, anyways. Unless they got lost, or they're retards.

EXT. BILLBOARD ROAD — DAY

Mildred interviewed by Gabriella, cameraman filming, all three billboards in the background.

> GABRIELLA
>
> This your first time on TV?

> MILDRED
>
> Uh-huh.

> GABRIELLA
>
> Well, don't be nervous, is the main thing, and it'll be fine. Just don't look into the camera, obviously.

Mildred just stares at her.

> In three, two, one. So, Mildred Hayes, why did you put up these billboards?

> MILDRED
>
> Well, my daughter, Angela, she got abducted, raped and murdered seven months ago, on this self-same stretch o' road here, and, to *me*, it seems like the local police department is too busy goin' round torturing black folks to be bothered doing anything about solving *actual* crime, so I kinda thought these here billboards might concentrate their minds some.

INT. DIXON'S HOUSE — NIGHT

Dixon sits beside his momma on the couch and is just to bite into a sandwich . . .

> DIXON
>
> Whatcha watching, Momma? The stupid news?

. . . when he's stopped by Mildred's appearance on TV.

> MILDRED
> (*on TV*)
>
> Seems like the local police department is too busy goin' round torturing black folks to be bothered doing anything about solving *actual* crime . . .

Dixon's momma looks at him.

> DIXON
> (*mouthing*)

Fuck.

INT. WILLOUGHBY HOUSE — NIGHT

Willoughby and Anne watching the end of the interview.

> MILDRED
> (*on TV*)

I don't know what these policemen are doing, to be honest with you. I just know my daughter's burnt body's lying six feet under the ground while they're eating Krispy Kremes and busting eight-year-olds for skateboarding in parking lots.

> GABRIELLA
> (*on TV*)

And what has Chief Willoughby to do with all this, why single him out?

> MILDRED
> (*on TV*)

Well, he's the head of 'em, ain't he? The buck's gotta stop at somebody, don't it?

> GABRIELLA
> (*on TV*)

And the buck stops at Willoughby?

> MILDRED
> (*on TV*)

Yeah, the buck stops at Willoughby. Dead right it does.

He clicks it off, gets up, goes out of the house without a word.

EXT. WILLOUGHBY'S STABLE — NIGHT

Willoughby moodily tending the horses in the stable just outside the house. Anne comes up.

ANNE

You alright there, fella?

WILLOUGHBY

Looks like we got a war on our hands.

EXT. MILDRED'S HOUSE — DAWN

Willoughby pulls up outside Mildred's poor, clapboard house. From here we can see that the billboards puncturing the dusty horizon are only a mile away. Mildred sees Willoughby from the kitchen window, as he knocks. She opens the door.

WILLOUGHBY

Can we talk?

EXT. MILDRED'S GARDEN — DAY

Mildred sitting on a creaky swing-set, Willoughby with hat in hand.

WILLOUGHBY

I'd do anything to catch the guy who did it, Mrs Hayes.
But when the DNA don't match no one who's ever been
arrested, and when the DNA don't match any other crime
nationwide, and when there wasn't a single eyewitness from
the time she left your house to the time we found her, well,
right now there ain't too much more that we can do,
except . . .

MILDRED

Could pull blood from every man and boy in this town,
over the age of eight.

WILLOUGHBY

There's civil rights laws prevents that, Mrs Hayes, and what
if he was just passing *through* town . . .

MILDRED

Pull blood from ever' man in the country, then.

WILLOUGHBY

And what if he was just passing through the country?

MILDRED

If it was *me*, I'd start up a database, every male baby what's born, stick 'em on it, cross-reference it, and as soon as they done something wrong, make a hundred-per-cent certain it was a correct match, then kill 'em.

WILLOUGHBY

Yeah, well, there's *definitely* civil rights laws prevents *that*.

He sits on the swing beside her, the billboards stretching out down the hill in front of them.

I'm doing everything I can to track him down, Mrs Hayes. I don't think those billboards is very fair.

MILDRED

The time it's took you to come out here whining like a bitch, Willoughby, some other poor girl's probably being butchered right now, but it's good you've got your priorities straight, I'll say that for ya.

WILLOUGHBY

There's something else, Mildred. (*Pause.*) I got cancer. I'm dying.

MILDRED

I know it.

WILLOUGHBY

Huh?

MILDRED

I know it. Most ever'body in town knows it.

WILLOUGHBY

You know it, and you still put those billboards up?

MILDRED

Well, they wouldn't be as effective after you croak, right?

Willoughby looks at her in disbelief, gets in his car, drives off.

INT. BAR – NIGHT

Town's main bar, Welby shooting pool against James, a local dwarf, who smacks a good one in from a distance. Dixon comes up, drunk.

> DIXON
>
> Well, looky looky, if it ain't the instigator of this whole goddam affair in the first place . . .

> RED
>
> I didn't instigate shit, Dixon . . .

> DIXON
>
> Playing pool against the town midget.

James pots another.

> JAMES
>
> He's right, Red, you *are* playing pool against the town midget.

> RED
>
> Well he's a *cop*, y'know, he's *observant*.

> DIXON
>
> You know, I always disliked you, Red, ever since you was a snotty little child, which you *still* look like. A snotty little child.

> RED
>
> Well that's unfortunate. I always thought you was great.

James plays a safety shot. Welby takes over.

> DIXON
>
> Even your name, 'Red Welby'. Even your name I disliked.

> RED
>
> Well . . . okay.

> DIXON
>
> Like you was some kind of a goddam Communist or something, and *proud* of it.

RED

No, it's cos I got red hair.

Welby misses.

DIXON

Do you know what they do to faggots down in Cuba, Welby?

RED

Wow, that's left-field . . . No, what do they do to faggots down in Cuba, Dixon?

DIXON

They kill 'em! Which, it might surprise you to learn, I am *against*.

RED

I'm not sure if they *do* kill faggots down in Cuba, Dixon. I know Cuba's human rights record is pretty deplorable when it comes to homosexuality, but killing 'em? Are you sure you ain't thinking of Wyoming?

DIXON

Always with the smart ass . . .

James smashes in another.

Jesus! He's quite good, isn't he? (*Pause.*) Willoughby's a good man, Red. He shouldn't have this be the only thing he thinks about, the last months left to him.

RED

The last months what?

DIXON

Oh. You didn't know. Yeah. Pancreatic.

Red is shaken. Out of nowhere, Mildred idles over, puts a bunch of quarters on the pool table.

MILDRED

I'm up next if any of you ole ladies ever quit *yakking*.

She hangs there, staring them down.

DIXON

Rude.

JAMES

Saw you on TV the other day, Mildred.

MILDRED

Oh yeah?

JAMES

Yeah, you looked good.

She stares at him. An embarrassed pause.

I mean, y'know, you came across really good, in the things
you were saying.

Embarrassed, James goes back to the pool.

DIXON

I didn't think you came across really good in the things you
were saying. I thought you came across as a stupid-ass.

MILDRED

Ain't it about time you got home to your momma, Dixon?

DIXON

No, it ain't time I got home to my momma. I tole her I was
gonna be out till twelve. Actually.

James whacks in the black brilliantly from a distance . . .

DIXON

Jesus!

JAMES

Me *v.* you, Mildred!

He smiles at her.

INT. MILDRED'S HOUSE – NIGHT

Mildred enters, a beer in hand, a bit drunk . . .

MILDRED

Hey Robbie? I think that midget wants to get in my pants –

. . . to find Father Montgomery, an old priest she knows, at the kitchen table beside Robbie, best teacups in front of them.

MILDRED

Father Montgomery.

FATHER MONTGOMERY

Mildred. I'm sorry for calling on you so late, although I must say Robbie's been the consummate host. Despite his having, he was just telling me, something of a tricky day at school.

ROBBIE

Oh, no, just some of the guys on the team was giving me crap.

MILDRED

Crap about what?

FATHER MONTGOMERY

About the billboards. Which is, uh, kind of what I've come to have a word with you about, Mildred.

MILDRED

Oh. Proceed.

FATHER MONTGOMERY

I know it's been hard for you, Mildred, this past year. We all do. The whole town does. And whatever it is you need, we'll be there for you. Always. But the town also knows what kind of a man William Willoughby is. And the town is dead set against these billboards of yours.

MILDRED

Took a poll, did ya, Father?

FATHER MONTGOMERY

If you hadn't stopped coming to church, Mildred, you'd be aware of the depth of people's feelings. I had a dozen people come up to me on Sunday. So, yes, I took a poll. Everybody is on your side about Angela. No one's on your side about this.

MILDRED

Y'know what I was thinking about, earlier today? I was thinking 'bout those street gangs they got in Los Angeles, the Crips and the Bloods? I was thinking about that buncha new laws they came up with, in the eighties I think it was, to combat those street gangs, those Crips and those Bloods. And, if I remember rightly, the gist of what those new laws said was, if you join one of these gangs, and you're running with 'em, and down the block from you one night, unbeknownst to you, your fellow Crips, or your fellow Bloods, shoot up a place, or stab a guy, well, even though you didn't know nothing about it, even though you may've just been standing on a street corner minding your own business, those new laws said you are *still culpable*. You are *still culpable*, by the very *act* of *joining* those Crips, or those Bloods, in the first place. Which got me thinking, Father, that whole type of situation is kinda similar to you Church boys, ain't it? You've got your colours, you've got your clubhouse, you're, for want of a better word, a gang. And if you're upstairs smoking a pipe and reading a Bible while one of your fellow gang members is downstairs fucking an altar boy then, Father, just like the Crips, and just like the Bloods, you're *culpable*. Cos you joined the gang, man. And I don't care if you never *did* shit or never *saw* shit or never *heard* shit. You joined the gang. You're culpable. And when a person is culpable to altar-boy-fucking, or *any*-kinda-boy-fucking, I know you guys didn't really narrow it down, then they kinda forfeit the right to come into my house and say a word about me, or my life, or my daughter, or my billboards. So, why don't you just finish up your tea there, Father, and get the fuck outta my kitchen.

She goes off to another room. Montgomery puts down his teacup.

ROBBIE
But thanks for coming up anyway, Father.

INT. HOSPITAL ROOM – DAY

Doctor drawing Willoughby's blood as he looks away from it, squeamish, out the window at the pretty landscape.

DOCTOR

How you been feeling, Bill?

WILLOUGHBY

Oh, like I got cancer in a major organ.

DOCTOR

Well, I just want you to know, we're all on your side about this Mildred Hayes thing . . .

WILLOUGHBY

If I have to hear that one more fucking time . . .!

He wrenches the needle from his arm, and tosses the vial at a wall, where it smashes and splatters.

I'm done with this shit. I can't waste my life waiting.

INT. POLICE STATION, MAIN ROOM — DAY

Willoughby breezes in, doing up his tie. Dixon's hungover.

WILLOUGHBY

Get me the file on the Hayes case.

DIXON

The Angela Hayes case or the Mildred Hayes case?

WILLOUGHBY

There *is* no Mildred Hayes case.

DIXON

We've had two official complaints about the billboards, so, actually . . .

WILLOUGHBY

From who?

DIXON
(*flipping through pad*)
A lady with a funny eye . . . and a fat dentist.

WILLOUGHBY

Get me the file on the *Angela* Hayes case. 'A lady with a funny fucking eye', Jesus Christ.

EXT. BILLBOARD ROAD — DAY

Backs of the billboards framed behind him, Willoughby has the case file laid out on the hood of his car, weighted with rocks. Some gruesome photos of a burnt corpse that we don't see much of but Dixon does, wincing, nauseous.

                    WILLOUGHBY
Late night?

                    DIXON
No.

                    WILLOUGHBY
Lay off that Welby guy.

                    DIXON
Or you'll do what?

                    WILLOUGHBY
Or I'll kick your momma's fucking teeth in.

                    DIXON
No, you won't. (*Pause.*) Who told ya I was laying *on* him anyway? The midget?

                    WILLOUGHBY
What the fuck are you talking about?! Fucking midgets! I'm trying to fucking concentrate!

Dixon shrugs. Willoughby goes back to the file. Dixon ambles, bored. Willoughby crouches, runs his fingers through the burnt soil there, looking like he might cry.

                    DIXON
What are you looking for, anyway? There's nothing to look for.

INT. DENTIST'S SURGERY — DAY

Mildred in a dentist's chair.

                    MILDRED
I don't know what it is. The filling feels like it's kinda waggling.

23

Geoffrey, a fat dentist, appears, with his instruments.

GEOFFREY
Well, if it's waggling it's gonna haveta come out.

MILDRED
(*bemused*)
Ain't you gonna have a look at it first?

Geoffrey does so, perfunctorily.

GEOFFREY
It's gonna haveta come out.

Bemused, she guesses he knows what he's doing. He fiddles among his drills, comes up with a high-pitched one.

MILDRED
Uh, can I get a little Novocaine, there, Doc?

He puts the drill down, gets a syringe, injects in under her gum at painful angles and length, takes it out and looks at his watch, just sitting there.

GEOFFREY
Give it a couple minutes.

Silence. Then he picks up the drill again, gets it going.

GEOFFREY
I just wanted to say . . . There's a lotta good friends of Bill Willoughby in this town, Mrs Hayes, who don't take kindly to . . .

But Mildred has already grabbed the drill hand, then grabbed the hand that was holding her mouth open. She slowly starts bringing one hand towards the other, the whirring drill aiming towards his big fat thumbnail.

Geoffrey is too flabby, and Mildred too forceful, for him to do anything about it but whimper, as . . .

Close up: the drill gets closer and closer to his thumbnail.

Geoffrey sweating . . .

Mildred determined . . .

. . . until finally the drill whirs into the nail, splitting it right down the centre.

MILDRED

Then why don't you tell those good friends of Bill Willoughby to tell him to go do his fucking job, fat boy.

She pushes the screaming bloody dentist out of the way, rinses her mouth out with the pink stuff, spits it at his head, and exits.

INT. GIFT SHOP — DAY

Denise behind counter, Mildred arranging knick-knacks. Cop car pulls up, lights flashing. Willoughby and Dixon enter.

WILLOUGHBY

Hey there, Mildred! You didn't happen to pay a visit to the dentist today, did ya?

Mildred's dialogue hereon is through a totally unintelligible, Novocained mouth.

MILDRED
(*unintelligibly*)

No.

WILLOUGHBY

Huh?

MILDRED
(*unintelligibly*)

Said 'No'.

WILLOUGHBY

Oh. So it wasn't you who drilled a little hole in one of big fat Geoffrey's big fat thumbnails, no?

MILDRED
(*unintelligibly*)

Of course not.

WILLOUGHBY

Huh?

MILDRED
(*unintelligibly*)
I said 'Of course not'.

DENISE
You drilled a hole in the dentist?

MILDRED
(*unintelligibly*)
No, Denise, I *didn't*.

WILLOUGHBY
Well, I thought it was kinda *funny* myself, but he wants to press charges, so we're gonna have to bring you in, I'm afraid.

INT. POLICE STATION, INTERVIEW ROOM – DAY

Dixon guarding door. Mildred looking out window.

Mildred's point-of-view: across the road, Welby and Pamela are looking out at the pedestrians in the sunshine. Welby's obviously into her, but shy about it. End point-of-view.

Mildred smiles. The Novocaine's worn off.

MILDRED
So how's it all going in the nigger-torturing business, Dixon?

DIXON
It's '*Persons* of *colour*'-torturing business, these days, if you want to know. And I didn't torture nobody.

She idles back to the table and sits.

Goddam saying that goddam stuff on TV. My momma watches that station!

MILDRED
And she didn't know nothing about the torturing?

DIXON
No, she didn't know anything about it. She's against that kinda thing.

26

Willoughby breezes in.

WILLOUGHBY
Who's against what kinda thing?

DIXON
My momma. Is against 'persons-of-colour torturing'. *She* said 'nigger-torturing'. *I* said you can't say 'nigger-torturing' no more. You gotta say 'persons-of-colour' torturing. Right?

WILLOUGHBY
I think I'll be able to take care of Mrs Hayes on my own from hereon, Jason.

DIXON
Sure, Chief, I'll be right outside if you need me.

Dixon gives Willoughby a pat on the back as he leaves. Willoughby sits with some papers.

WILLOUGHBY
Don't gimme that look. If you got rid of every cop with vaguely racist leanings then you'd have three cops left and all o' them are gonna hate the fags so what are ya gonna do, y'know?

He smiles at Mildred, then comes round and sits on her side of the desk, looking down on her.

I wanna know something, Mildred. Why'd ya drill a hole through poor fat Geoffrey's thumbnail?

MILDRED
Oh, that didn't happen. His hand slipped and he drilled a hole through his own self. Is he saying I done it? Jeez, then I guess it's just his word against mine, huh? Kinda like in all those rape cases you hear about. Except, in this case, the chick ain't losing.

WILLOUGHBY
It ain't really about winning or losing, though, is it, Mildred? I mean, do you think *I* care about who wins or loses between the two of yous? Do you think I care about *dentists*? I don't care about *dentists*. *Nobody* cares about

27

dentists! I *do* care about, or I'm *interested in*, tying you up
in court so long that your hours at the gift shop are so shot
to shit that you ain't got a penny to pay for another month's
billboards. I'm interested in *that*.

MILDRED

I got some dough put away . . .

WILLOUGHBY

What *I* heard was you had to sell off your ex-husband's
tractor-trailer to even pay for *this* month's billboards, that
right? (*Pause.*) How is ole Charlie, by the way? He still
shacked up with that pretty little intern works down at the
zoo?

MILDRED

He's still shacked up with some chick who smells of shit. I
don't know if the zoo's got anything to do with it. Although
I'd *hope* so.

WILLOUGHBY

How old is she? Nineteen? That must smart.

MILDRED

Keep trying, Officer. Keep trying.

WILLOUGHBY

What's Charlie think about these here billboards of yours,
an ex-cop like Charlie?

MILDRED

Ex-cop, ex-wife-beater. Same difference, I guess, right?

WILLOUGHBY

His word against yours, though, right? (*Pause.*) Charlie
don't know about them, does he?

MILDRED

It's none of his business.

WILLOUGHBY

He's kinda paying for 'em though, ain't he?

MILDRED

I'm paying for 'em.

WILLOUGHBY

This month you are. How about when . . .

Willoughby suddenly lets out a short sharp cough which spurts a spray of blood that hits Mildred in the face, wholly by accident. Horrified, shaking, Willoughby tries to wipe her face with a handkerchief, Mildred almost in tears at his embarrassment.

WILLOUGHBY

I didn't mean to . . .

MILDRED

I know . . .

WILLOUGHBY

It was an accident . . .

MILDRED

I know, baby.

WILLOUGHBY

It's blood.

They're both in tears, and there's a desperation in his eyes, as he sits there shaking.

MILDRED

I'll go get somebody . . .

She rushes out the door.

EXT. POLICE STATION — DAY

Willoughby is gurneyed into an ambulance past townspeople, Dixon beside him.

WILLOUGHBY

Just let her go.

Dixon rolls his eyes.

Just let her go!

Dixon nods as the ambulance doors close.

INT. CAR – DUSK

Mildred driving Robbie home from school.

> ROBBIE

Do birds get cancer?

> MILDRED

Huh?

> ROBBIE

Birds. Do they get cancer?

> MILDRED

I don't know. Dogs do.

> ROBBIE

Yeah, well, I wasn't talking about dogs, was I?

The car turns on to the billboard road.

Great, the good ole 'Raped While Dying' route home. Cos if there was two seconds in a day when I *didn't* think about her, and *wasn't* thinking about how she died, 'There ya go, Robbie, think about it some more, why don't ya?' It's good, too, that as much as a person might've tried to avoid the details of what happened, cos he didn't think it'd do any *good*, and he didn't think he could *bear* it, it's also good to be informed in twenty-foot-high lettering, and a real nice *font*, the precise *details* of her last moments, y'know? That it wasn't enough that she was raped, and it wasn't enough that she died, no. 'Raped While Dying'. Thank you, Mom.

> MILDRED

I gave you the police reports . . .

> ROBBIE

I didn't read 'em! I'm depressed enough as it fucking is!

INT. MILDRED'S HOUSE – NIGHT

Robbie slams into his room, leaving Mildred alone and quiet. She goes into Angela's room, sits on the bed a while.

ANGELA
(*off screen*)

Mom?

MILDRED
(*off screen*)

Yeah?

INT. MILDRED'S HOUSE, KITCHEN — DAY

Flashback. It's ten months ago. Mildred washing dishes. Robbie drawing, Angela dressed to go out.

ANGELA
You ain't going out again tonight, are ya?

MILDRED
Denise said we might get us a coupla drinks later, yeah.

ANGELA
Denise gonna be driving ya?

MILDRED
Angela, why don't you just ask me if you can borrow the car?

ANGELA
Can I borrow the car?

MILDRED

No.

ANGELA

Bitch!

MILDRED
But I'll give you money for a taxi if you ask me nice and don't call me a bitch.

ANGELA
Why did you make me ask you borrow it if you was never gonna let me borrow it?

MILDRED
Cos it was funny. And cos you've been smoking pot all day.

31

ANGELA

You are such a hypocrite!

MILDRED

'Hypocrite', how?

ANGELA

You drove drunk with us in the car when we was kids.

MILDRED

What are you talking about?

ANGELA

Daddy told me.

MILDRED

(*pause*)

When did you see him?

ANGELA

I see him all the time, don't change the subject. Did you
or did you not drive drunk with us in the car when we
was kids?

MILDRED

Once, maybe . . .

ANGELA

Oh, 'once', okay . . .

MILDRED

When he was in the middle of beating the shit out of me . . .

ANGELA

Which we've only got your word about, right?

ROBBIE

For Christ's sake, Angela . . .

ANGELA

Oh, why are you never on my side, Robbie?

ROBBIE

I'm always on your side when you're not being a cunt.

ANGELA

Hey!

MILDRED

(*same time*)

Hey . . . ! There'll be no more 'cunts' in this house, you got that, mister?

ROBBIE

What, are you moving out?

Both women glare at him.

It was a gag!

ANGELA

So are ya gonna let me borrow the car or what?

MILDRED

Why don't you just walk, Angela? Why don't you just walk?

ANGELA

You know what, I *will* walk, I *will* walk. And y'know what? I hope I get raped on the way.

Angela storms out . . .

MILDRED

Yeah? Well I hope you get raped on the way too!

Door slams, flashback over.

INT. HOSPITAL ROOM – NIGHT

Willoughby in a bed, Anne nearby, Doctor checking him.

DOCTOR

We're gonna need to keep you in a few days, Bill. You shouldn't be coughing up blood.

WILLOUGHBY

Yeah, I kinda guessed that, Doc.

DOCTOR

I'll swing by in the morning, Anne.

Doctor departs, and we listen to his echoing footsteps as they look at each other.

> ANNE
>
> Guess I'll go get your coat, huh?

> WILLOUGHBY
>
> Well you *know* I ain't staying . . .

> ANNE
>
> And you *know* I ain't arguing.

She smiles and goes out, footsteps echo away, leaving him alone there, in the sterile quiet. Scared.

EXT. MILDRED'S HOUSE – DAWN

A pretty pink sunrise over the hills behind the house.

INT. MILDRED'S HOUSE, KITCHEN – DAY

Mildred and Robbie getting their breakfasts in silence, Robbie more moody than she is. She tries to make him laugh, he ignores her. Finally, she takes a big spoonful of milk and cereal and slings it straight in his face and hair.

> MILDRED
>
> Slipped. Oops.

She stares at him, deadpan, as milk and cereal drip down his face and hair.

> ROBBIE
>
> You . . . old . . . cunt.

> MILDRED
> (*suppressing laughter*)
>
> I ain't old, Robbie.

Robbie can't help but smile, then hears the sound of a car pulling up on the gravel outside.

> ROBBIE
>
> That's Dad.

He wipes his face, rushes to the door, Mildred apprehensive.

EXT. MILDRED'S HOUSE — CONTINUOUS

Her ex, Charlie, slams his car door shut and approaches the front door as Robbie opens it. Charlie's nineteen-year-old girlfriend, Penelope, remains in the passenger seat.

ROBBIE

Hey, Dad! How you doing?

CHARLIE

Where's the crazy lady . . .?

Robbie gestures inside and Charlie breezes in. Robbie waves to Penelope, who smiles and gives an embarrassed wave back.

INT. MILDRED'S HOUSE, KITCHEN — CONTINUOUS

Robbie, Charlie and Mildred, who's still finishing breakfast.

CHARLIE

The kid's got Rice fucking Krispies in his fucking hair! What's going on around here? And what the fuck's going on with these fucking billboards, Mildred?

MILDRED

Kinda self-explanatory, ain't it?

CHARLIE

Well, why don't you just explain it to me?

MILDRED

Guess it *ain't* self-explanatory then. Well, y'know, I guess I wanted certain people's *minds* kept on certain people's *jobs*, is all. I hadn't heard a word from 'em in seven goddam months, but I tell ya this, I heard an awful lot from 'em since I put those billboards up . . .

CHARLIE

You think this has focused their minds? I'll tell you what it's focused their minds on. It's focused their minds on how exactly are they gonna *fuck you up.*

MILDRED

The more you keep a case in the public eye, the better your chances of getting it solved, it's in all the guidebooks, Charlie.

CHARLIE

How much those billboards cost?

MILDRED

'Bout the same as a tractor-trailer.

Robbie sniggers.

CHARLIE

What the fuck are you laughing at?

ROBBIE

Nothing.

CHARLIE

Laughed at by a guy with fucking cereal in his hair!

ROBBIE

How's Penelope?

CHARLIE

Huh? She's alright.

ROBBIE

Why don't you invite her in, save leaving her sitting there?

MILDRED

She's here?

CHARLIE

She's out in the car.

MILDRED

Oh. That explains it.

CHARLIE

That explains what?

MILDRED

I *knew* I could smell *something*.

Charlie overturns the table violently and, as Mildred backs away, grabs her by the neck and pins her against the wall. Just as suddenly, a knife is placed against Charlie's throat by Robbie, deadly serious.

ROBBIE

Let her go.

Just then, the sound of a screen door creaking is heard, and Penelope is standing there, startled by the scene.

PENELOPE

Oh, um, I kinda needed to use the bathroom, but if it's inconvenient, actually it *is* inconvenient, isn't it, I can see it's inconvenient, I can hold it, it's alright . . .

Charlie lets go of Mildred and Robbie lowers the knife.

ROBBIE

It's the first door, down the hall.

PENELOPE

Are you sure? I feel like I'm intruding . . .

CHARLIE

Just go pee!

Penelope quickly heads down the hall to the toilet, leaving the three of them staring at each other. Robbie sets right the upturned table.

MILDRED

Look, you've said what you came to say. Okay? Why don't ya just go get zoo girl and get the hell out of my house? Alright?

Penelope comes out of the toilet.

PENELOPE

Um, actually, zoo-wise, they were letting people go at the zoo, unfortunately, and it was a case of 'last in, first out', so, yeah, unfortunately the zoo had to let me go. But they were looking for people down at the horse-rides for the disableds, to look after the horses down there, so I'm working down there now, looking after the disableds' horses . . .

Pause. Charlie nods for her to go. She exits.

CHARLIE
Don't say a word.

MILDRED
I wasn't gonna say a word.

CHARLIE
Don't you think *I* don't wish it had never happened?! Don't you think *I* don't wish she was here still?!

MILDRED
I know you do. I know you do.

CHARLIE
Billboards ain't gonna bring her back, Mildred.

MILDRED
Neither is fucking nineteen-year-olds, Charlie.

CHARLIE
Yeah. But I *know* that.

MILDRED
(*pause*)

Just go.

CHARLIE
Yeah, alright, I'm such a shitty dad and you're such a great mom. Alright. So how come a week before she died she comes around asking if she can move in with me at my place, cos she couldn't stand the two of yous bitching at each other no more, and fighting with each other no more?

MILDRED
I don't believe you . . .

CHARLIE
And I said 'No, stay at home, your mom loves you.' And now I wish I hadn't, cos if I hadn't she'd still fucking be here!

MILDRED
I don't believe you!

CHARLIE
Don't believe me. Ask Fruit Loop boy.

Charlie leaves. Sound of his car pulling away.

MILDRED

Is it true?

ROBBIE

I don't know, Mom.

MILDRED

Yeah, you do.

INT. DIXON'S HOUSE – DAY

Dixon beside his momma on couch. He's got his tortoise on his lap, she pours a margarita from a ready-made plastic pack. They're watching on TV the start of Don't Look Now.

DIXON

Oh, not Donald Sutherland again! What *is* this, a freaking Donald Sutherland season?!

MOMMA

I like him. I like his hair.

DIXON

Hair!

MOMMA

This is the one where his little girl dies.

DIXON

Always a plus in a movie! (*Pause.*) It any good?

MOMMA

It's got a great sex scene.

Dixon gives her an uncomfortable glance.

MOMMA

Talking of dead kids, what's happening with the billboard lady?

DIXON

Oh, that cooze won't listen to reason. She's as tough as an old boot!

MOMMA

Oh. Why don't you just fuck her over through her friends then?

DIXON

Huh?

MOMMA

Y'know, why don't you fuck her friends over? Make her come around that way. Has she got some friends you could fuck over?

Dixon thinks about it, nods.

EXT. GIFT SHOP — DAY

Mildred finds the shop shut. A handwritten note on it reads 'I got arrested! Denise!' With an unsmiley face.

INT. POLICE STATION, MAIN ROOM — DAY

Desk Sergeant sighs as Mildred enters. Dixon is some desks away across the crowded station.

MILDRED
(*shouted at Dixon*)

Hey, fuckhead?!

Every cop turns to look at her, the audacity of it . . .

DIXON

What?

DESK SERGEANT

Don't say 'What?', Dixon, when she comes in calling you a fuckhead, and don't *you* come in here . . .

MILDRED

Shut up! (*To Dixon.*) You! Get over here.

DIXON

No. *You* get over *here.*

40

MILDRED

Alright . . .

She heads over to Dixon.

DESK SERGEANT

What?! Don't . . . *Dixon!*

DIXON

What?! I'm taking care of this!

DESK SERGEANT

You do not allow a member of the public to call you a
fuckhead in the station house!

DIXON

That's what I'm doing, I'm taking care of it! In my *own
way. Actually.* Now get out of my ass!

Desk Sergeant sighs and goes back to work.

DIXON

Mrs Hayes. What is it I can do for you today?

MILDRED

Where's Denise Watson?

DIXON

Denise Watson's in the clank.

MILDRED

On what charge?

DIXON

Possession.

MILDRED

Of what?

DIXON

Two marijuana cigarettes. Big ones.

MILDRED

When's the bail hearing?

DIXON

I asked the judge not to give her bail on account of her
previous marijuana violations and the judge said sure.

MILDRED

You fucking prick.

DIXON

You do *not* call an officer of the *law* a fucking *prick* in his
own *station house*, Mrs Hayes. Or *anywhere*, actually.

MILDRED
(leaving)

What's with the new hard-boiled attitude, Dixon? Your
momma been coaching ya?

DIXON

No. My momma doesn't do that.

Mildred passes Desk Sergeant on the way out.

Take 'em down, Hayes!

She's gone.

DESK SERGEANT

You did good, Dixon.

DIXON

Yeah, I know I did.

Desk Sergeant just sighs.

EXT. BEAUTIFUL MEADOW BESIDE LAKE – DAY

*Anne is looking confused, glass of wine in hand. The kids in the middle
of a blanket on the grass, holding a child's magnetic fishing rod each.
Willoughby tosses teddy bears and dolls two metres away from the
circumference of the blanket.*

WILLOUGHBY

Now, the rules here are twofold; no kid can leave this
goddam blanket at any goddam time, and every single one
of these dolls and these teddy bears has gotta be hooked

42

up. Now, your momma and I, although it won't look like it, we'll be watching every goddam move you make and the most important thing while we're watching you is you do not leave this blanket. The next most important thing is you do not at any stage allow the fishing rods to stick into you or your sister's eyeballs, as this would be counter-productive to the entire operation. What would this be?

BOTH GIRLS
(*stumbling*)

'Counter-productive to the entire operation.'

WILLOUGHBY

Good. Then troops . . . start fishing.

They do so, as Willoughby grabs a blanket, a bottle of wine, takes Anne by the hand and leads her uphill to the treeline.

ANNE

We. Are. Not.

WILLOUGHBY

We are.

She looks back at the kids, safe within the confines of the blanket, and lets herself be led.

EXT. BILLBOARD ROAD — DAY

Mildred fixing flowers in pots at the billboards, making them look nice. It's a beautiful, blue-skied day; pretty birds mooch around, and out of nowhere a fawn suddenly appears.

Mildred stays dead still, breathless at the beauty of it, watching as it almost appears to look up at AND STILL NO ARRESTS *and cock its head at the question. It spots Mildred suddenly and is startled slightly, but stands its ground.*

MILDRED

Hey, baby. Yep, still no arrests. How come, I wonder? Cos there ain't no God and the whole world's empty and it don't matter what we do to each other? Ooh, I hope not. (*Pause.*) How comes you came up here outta nowhere, looking so

43

pretty? You ain't trying to make me believe in reincarnation or something, are ya? Well, you're pretty, but you ain't her. She got killed, and now she'll be dead forever. I do thank you for coming up, though. If I had some food I'd give it ya, but I've only got some Doritos and I'd be scared they'd kill ya, they're kinda pointy. Then where would we be?

The fawn finally decides to amble away, off towards the hazy sunset horizon. She almost cries but doesn't quite.

MILDRED

Oh Mildred.

INT. WELBY'S OFFICE – DAY

Mildred sitting at desk, Welby idling shiftily by the window.

RED

Yeah, so I, uh, just happened to be looking over our contract we drew up back that time, and what I realised was, I realised that although payment is to be made on the first day of each month, uh, the first payment *you* paid was actually a deposit, wasn't it, like we said, so actually, in point of fact, you're actually *behind* in your payments now, by, yeah, a month.

She gives him a look.

Yeah. That's, uh, what the contract says. Looking it over an' all. The lawyer says so too.

MILDRED

When do you need this next payment by, Red?

RED

Uh, well, *now*, really.

Another look.

Or Fuh— uh . . . Friday?

MILDRED

Wow. When you can't trust the lawyers and the advertising men, what the hell's America coming to, huh? (*Pause.*) Who got to ya? Willoughby?

44

RED

Nobody got to me.

MILDRED

My fat fucking ass!

RED

He's *dying*, Mildred.

MILDRED

We're *all* fucking dying!

Pamela knocks at the door.

PAMELA

Red?

RED

Oh, hi Pamela! Um, we're a little bit busy, at the moment, Pam, if that's okay.

PAMELA

Oh Red, I know, and I know you were real anxious about talking to Mrs Hayes this morning and all . . .

RED

Anxious? No.

PAMELA

But that's the thing, there's no need to be, cos you won't *believe* it! A little Mexican delivery boy just dropped in with this . . .

Pamela hands Welby an envelope, full of banknotes.

RED

What the hell's this?!

PAMELA

I know! It's five thousand dollars! And guess what the note says? It says it's to pay for the rental on Mrs Hayes' billboards! Can you believe it? That's why I butted in!

RED

Well, who's it from?

45

PAMELA

Well, it doesn't say.

RED

Well, where's the delivery boy?

PAMELA

Well, he went.

RED

Well, did you see what company he was from?

PAMELA

Well, no.

RED

Well, what kinda uniform did he have on?

PAMELA

Well, he just looked like one of those fat little Mexican boys. (*Pause.*) On a bicycle? (*Pause.*) Did I do something wrong?

RED

No, Pam, you did good.

MILDRED

Yeah, Pam, you did *real* good.

PAMELA

Did I? Great! Ain't life crazy?

Pamela smiles, gives Red the thumbs-up, leaves.

MILDRED

What's the note say?

RED

Says, er, 'This here money is to go towards the fund for Mildred Hayes' billboards, cos she ain't the only one round here who hates the pigs. Signed, a friend.'

MILDRED

Jeez, I guess ya can't be picky who your friends are these days, huh? (*Standing.*) Um, be good to get a little receipt off

46

ya, Red, y'know, saying the price of next month's is paid in
full an' all.

                        RED

Oh. Sure, Mildred, sure.

                      MILDRED

Yeah. Like, *now*.

                        RED

Oh! Sure!

Welby hurriedly writes one out.

INT. WILLOUGHBY HOUSE — NIGHT

Willoughby tucks the kids in as they giggle.

                        JANE

Is Mommy drunk, Daddy?

                     WILLOUGHBY

No, no, she's just got a little migraine, that's all. A little
Chardonnay migraine, now no more chit-chat out of you
two, okay?

                        JANE

Can we stay home from school again tomorrow, Daddy?

                     WILLOUGHBY

We'll see what your mommy says in the morning, darling . . .

                    JANE/POLLY

Aww!

                     WILLOUGHBY

Now eyes closed and get some sleep, okay?

He kisses them goodnight, switches the light off.

INT. WILLOUGHBY LIVING ROOM — CONTINUOUS

*Anne is lying on the couch, a small wet towel over her eyes. Willoughby
sits in beside her and kisses her.*

WILLOUGHBY

You don't smell of puke. Which is good.

ANNE

Aquafresh. Trick I learned.

WILLOUGHBY

Women, huh?

ANNE

Oh yeah. Resourceful.

WILLOUGHBY

It's still your turn to clean the horseshit outta the stable, y'know?

ANNE

Oh those fucking horses! They're *your* fucking horses! I'm gonna have those fucking horses shot!

WILLOUGHBY

I'll do it, you lazy bitch.

ANNE

Thank you, Poppa. (*Pause.*) That was a real nice day. And that was a real nice fuck. You got a real nice cock, Mr Willoughby.

WILLOUGHBY

Is that from a play, 'You got a real nice cock, Mr Willoughby'? I think I heard it in a Shakespeare one time.

ANNE

You dummy. It's Oscar Wilde.

She puts the towel back over her eyes as he laughs.

INT. WILLOUGHBY'S STABLE — NIGHT

The horses watch as he finishes shovelling the shit, lays out fresh hay, gives them a pat, thinks about the day, smiles.

WILLOUGHBY

'Oscar Wilde.'

He smiles again, then picks up a black hood, on the outside of which he has pinned a note that reads 'Don't open the bag. Just telephone the boys.'

He places the black hood snugly over his head so the note is visible, cocks a large hand gun, raises the gun to his temple, and shoots himself through the head. His dead body falls heavily to the ground, the hood concealing all the mess.

INT. WILLOUGHBY HOUSE – CONTINUOUS

Anne pulls the towel off her eyes, having heard something. She gets up and we go with her, camera on her face, as she moves all the way through the house to the kitchen, where she stops suddenly, and her face falls . . .

                    ANNE
No. No. No . . . !

We see what she sees – a plain white envelope propped on the bare kitchen table, the single word 'Anne' dead centre of it.

No! No! No! No!

She breaks down crying on the cold kitchen floor.

We hear Willoughby's note over the following silent images:

INT. WILLOUGHBY HOUSE – NIGHT

Polly and Jane framed in their dark doorway, as their mother cries on the floor;

EXT. WILLOUGHBY'S STABLE – NIGHT

The horses bemused in Willoughby's garden, as Anne stands drained in the doorway of the stable, the crescent moon above it. She slowly trudges back to the house;

INT. WILLOUGHBY HOUSE – NIGHT

Anne lying on Jane's bed, hugging Polly and Jane to her, all eyes open, numb, as a uniformed cop stands guard outside the room and other cops move through the house;

EXT. BEAUTIFUL MEADOW BESIDE LAKE — NIGHT

The beautiful lakeside in the moonlight, and the one teddy bear laying there that they missed, its grumpy little face;

EXT. WILLOUGHBY'S STABLE — NIGHT

Flashing lights, the cops and ambulance people at the stable;

Blood seeping along the 'Just telephone the boys' part of the note (so only the words 'The Just' aren't blood-covered). The Desk Sergeant winces as he opens the hood.

INT. WILLOUGHBY HOUSE — NIGHT

Willoughby quietly finishing the note at the kitchen table, Anne's drunken feet, in fun socks, visible on the distant couch. He puts it in an envelope marked 'Anne', gets up, and quietly leaves the house;

> WILLOUGHBY
> (*voice-over*)
> My darling Anne. There's a longer letter in the dresser drawer I've been writing for the last week or so. That one covers us, and my memories of us, and how much I've always loved you. This one just covers tonight, and, more importantly, today. Tonight I have gone out to the horses to end it. I cannot say sorry for the act itself, although I know that for a short time you will be angry at me or even hate me for it. Please don't. This is not a case of 'I came in this world alone, and I'm going out of it alone' or anything dumb like that. I did not come in this world alone, my mom was there, and I am not going out of it alone, cos you are there, drunk on the couch, making Oscar Wilde cock jokes. No. This is a case, in some senses, of bravery. Not the bravery of facing a bullet down; the next few months of pain would be far harder than that small flash. No, it's the bravery of weighing up the next few months of still being

with you, still waking up with you, of playing with the kids, against the next few months of seeing in your eyes how much my pain is killing you; how my weakened body as it ebbs away and you tend to it are your final and lasting memories of me. I won't have that. Your final memories of me will be us at the riverside, and that dumb fishing game (which I think they cheated at), and me inside of you, and you on top of me, and barely a fleeting thought of the darkness yet to come. That was the best, Anne. A whole day of not thinking about it. Dwell on this day, baby, cos it was the best day of my life. Kiss the girls for me, and know that I've always loved you, and maybe I'll see you again if there's another place. And if there ain't, well, it's been Heaven knowing you. Your boy, Bill.

EXT. POLICE STATION — DAY

Early morning on Main Street. Dixon can be seen through his window, iPod earphones on.

INT. POLICE STATION, MAIN ROOM — DAY

Dixon at his desk, first one in, singing along quietly to Abba's 'Chiquitita'.

Cops start coming in on the other side of room, and the ones who aren't in tears are when they're told. Dixon is oblivious to all this, and because we're with his music, we don't hear the sound of it either.

Dixon looks up and finally notices something is amiss when he sees a fellow cop smashing a chair to pieces and being restrained by the Desk Sergeant and two other cops, as he breaks down in tears. Dixon takes his earphones out.

> DIXON
> (*laughing*)
> What the hell's going on around here?

All the cops turn and look at him.

> What?

INT. POLICE STATION, TOILET — DAY

Desk Sergeant holds Dixon up at the sink he's slumped at, nose streaming, crying quietly, dizzy.

> DESK SERGEANT
> Can you stand now?

> DIXON
> I can stand, I can stand . . .

> DESK SERGEANT
> I'd better get out there, say something to 'em. You ain't gonna faint again, are ya?

Dixon shakes his head. Desk Sergeant goes out. Dixon cleans himself up, looks at himself in the mirror, breathes deeply, exits.

INT. POLICE STATION, MAIN ROOM — DAY

Dixon pulls on his jacket and looks out his window as the Desk Sergeant speaks . . .

Point-of-view: out of window. In his second-storey window, Welby sits at his desk, chatting with Pamela, who laughs at a joke he's made. End point-of-view.

> DESK SERGEANT
> . . . that the best thing, the only thing, to honour that man's memory right now, is to go to work. Is to be a good cop. Is to walk in his shoes. Is to do what he did, every day of his life. *Help* people.

Dixon straps on his belt, picks up his night stick and walks out of the station. We track him in one continuous shot . . .

EXT. POLICE STATION — CONTINUOUS

. . . as he walks across the street, cars screeching to a halt, to Welby's building. He smashes its glass door with his night stick and carries on through it, and we continue tracking him . . .

INT. WELBY'S BUILDING – CONTINUOUS

. . . as he walks up the stairs to the second floor, to Welby in the office, startled at the glass smashing. He backs away from him . . .

RED

What the hell's going on, Dixon?

Dixon clubs Welby in the face and Welby goes down, Pamela screaming. Dixon continues calmly to the window, smashes it with the night stick, picks Welby up and shoves him out of it.

Welby disappears out the window, his screams remaining for a second till they're ended with a sickening thud.

PAMELA

You fucking pig! What the fuck are you doing?!

Dixon clubs Pamela across the face, breaking her nose. She collapses, and he walks all the way back downstairs and into the street, and we continue to track him, as . . .

EXT. MAIN STREET – DAY

. . . he comes out, sees Welby, broken ankle/arm/hand, trying to get up and crawl away. Dixon comes up behind, clubs him back down . . .

DIXON

See, Red? I got issues with *white* folks too . . .

Dixon calmly walks back into the police station, passing a well-dressed black man, Abercrombie, on his way.

DIXON

The fuck are you looking at?

Dixon enters the station. Abercrombie lowers his coffee, and we see his cop's badge as he takes in the carnage on the street. End of tracking shot.

INT. MILDRED'S HOUSE, KITCHEN – DAY

Mildred and Robbie, fixing cornflakes and coffee, TV on in background. The local news flashes back on, an image of Willoughby, the Anchor announcing . . .

ANCHOR (TV)

Reports, sadly, have come in overnight, that Chief William Willoughby of Ebbing, Missouri, took his own life early this morning . . .

Mildred reacts like she's been punched . . .

. . . in the grounds of his home. This report just in from Gabriella Forrester.

TV cuts to Gabriella (who interviewed Mildred weeks back) outside the Willoughby home, yellow cordon tape up, etc.

GABRIELLA (TV)

Tragedy came calling today upon this quiet family home outside of Ebbing, Missouri; a home belonging to Chief William Willoughby, his wife, Anne, his two young daughters, Polly and Jane. What appears to be a self-inflicted gunshot wound brought life to an end for Chief Willoughby, a man highly-respected in Ebbing for his diligence and his service to the community, a service that lasted more than twenty-five years. What led him to take his life in the early hours of this morning it is too early to speculate; there were rumours of illness; could it simply have been the pressure of the job; or could it have something to do with a story we ran here just two weeks ago, of these billboards, and the woman who put them there, Mildred Hayes . . .

Mildred flips the TV off with the remote.

EXT. SCHOOL – DAY

Robbie gets out of the car as a group of two boys and one girl stare over at Mildred. Suddenly a can of Coke hits the windscreen, from their direction. Mildred looks at the fizz.

ROBBIE

Don't.

Mildred gets out of the car, walks over to one of the boys.

MILDRED

Say, do you know who threw that can?

BOY

What can?

Mildred kicks him hard in the crotch. He goes down. She turns to the girl next to him.

MILDRED

How about you, honey? Do you know who threw that can?

GIRL

Uh, no, I didn't really see . . .

Mildred kicks her hard in the crotch. She goes down. She stares at the other boy, who kinda shudders. She goes back to the car, gets in, speeds off.

ROBBIE
(*under breath*)

Thanks, Mom.

INT. POLICE STATION, MAIN ROOM — DAY

Dixon's fellow cops slap him on the back in praise, as Abercrombie quietly enters and walks up to the Desk Sergeant.

DESK SERGEANT

And what can I do for *you* today, sir?

ABERCROMBIE

What's your name?

DESK SERGEANT

Name's on my tag, man. You hard of reading?

ABERCROMBIE

Hard of reading, no, no. That's good, 'hard of reading'. It's kind of like 'hard of hearing', but it's actually 'hard of reading', it's like a play on words or something.

DESK SERGEANT

What do you *want*?

ABERCROMBIE

Uh, I've been sent down to uh, take over from Chief Willoughby, in light of last night's unfortunate event.

DIXON
(*from back of room*)
You have got to be fucking kidding me!

DESK SERGEANT
Do you have any documentation to prove that, sir?

ABERCROMBIE
You really wanna see my documentation, fucker?

Abercrombie stares at him, cold as ice.

DIXON
Yeah, see his documentation!

Desk Sergeant backs down. Abercrombie strolls up to Dixon's desk, all the other cops watching.

ABERCROMBIE
(*to the others*)
None o' you cracker motherfuckers got no work to do?

Cops go back to work.

DIXON
(*quietly*)
Ain't that racialist?

Abercrombie sits on Dixon's desk.

ABERCROMBIE
What happened to your hands there, Officer Dixon?

DIXON
Oh, I just kinda banged 'em up a little bit while I was throwing some guy out of a fucking window. Y'know, the usual.

ABERCROMBIE
Oh yeah? They never taught me *that* one at the Academy.

DIXON
Which fucking Academy *you* go to?

Abercrombie looks over Dixon's cluttered desk; his momma's photo, toy figurines, Angela Hayes' case file, a comic book.

ABERCROMBIE

How's things coming along on the Angela Hayes case?

DIXON

How's things coming along on the 'Mind your own fucking business' case?

ABERCROMBIE

How's things coming along on the hand me your gun and your badge?

Dixon snorts, then, as he realises he means it, is sickened.

DIXON

Huh?

ABERCROMBIE

Hand me your gun and your badge.

Dixon's eyes well up. Abercrombie just stares right past him. Dixon gives Abercrombie his gun, then checks himself for his badge. He can't find it. He goes through all his pockets, embarrassed, as Abercrombie waits. Still can't find it.

DIXON

I can't find my badge. No, seriously. Maybe I dropped it when I was doing the window guy?

ABERCROMBIE

Just get the fuck out of my station house, man.

Dixon rises, sadly. Looks to his fellow cops. Who look away. Abercrombie enters Willoughby's office, slams the door behind him. Dixon shuffles up to the Desk Sergeant.

DIXON

I think I just got fired. Fired or suspended, I'm not sure which . . .

DESK SERGEANT

Fired.

Dixon looks at him, eyes welling up. He nods, and leaves before he starts crying.

INT. GIFT SHOP — DAY

A pick-up truck pulls up outside. Mildred, reading a magazine, watches as a well-built, Crop-Haired Guy, late twenties, enters, kinda stares straight at her a moment, then ambles around the shop, looking at knick-knacks he obviously has no use for.

> MILDRED
>
> Anything I can help you with, just gimme a holler.

> CROP-HAIRED GUY
> (*pause*)
>
> Give you a what?

> MILDRED
>
> A holler?

He stares at her again, then continues with the knick-knacks.

> CROP-HAIRED GUY
>
> A holler, huh? (*Pause.*) Give Mildred Hayes a holler. Okay.

> MILDRED
>
> You know me?

> CROP-HAIRED GUY
>
> Only from the TV, and the radio. How much these here 'Welcome to Missouri' rabbits go for?

> MILDRED
>
> Seven bucks. It's writ right on 'em.

Guy tosses a glass rabbit against a distant shelf, where it, and the things on the shelf, shatter, startling Mildred.

> CROP-HAIRED GUY
>
> Guess he ain't seven bucks now.

> MILDRED
>
> What the hell was it you come in here for?

> CROP-HAIRED GUY
>
> What did I come in here for? Well, maybe I'm a good friend of Willoughby's, how about that?

MILDRED

Are you?

CROP-HAIRED GUY

Or, y'know . . . maybe I was a friend of your daughter's or something. How about that?

MILDRED

(*pause*)

Were you?

CROP-HAIRED GUY

Or, uh, y'know, maybe I was the guy who fucked her while she was dying? How about that?

They stare at each other a while.

MILDRED

Were you?

CROP-HAIRED GUY

Oh . . . Naw. I would've *liked* to. I saw her picture in the paper there.

Doorbell tinkles, as Anne enters, dressed in black.

CROP-HAIRED GUY

Saved by the bell, huh?

Guy turns to leave.

MILDRED

You owe me seven fucking dollars for the rabbit.

CROP-HAIRED GUY

Guess you'll have to get it off me next time I'm passing through, huh, Mildred?

MILDRED

I guess I will.

Guy exits. Anne, who she's never seen before, comes up.

You don't know how glad I am to see you.

ANNE

What?!

MILDRED

That guy was scaring me.

ANNE

I wouldn't have said you scare easy.

MILDRED

I ain't the worst. What can I do for you, ma'am?

ANNE

My husband left this for you before he shot himself in the head last night.

Anne hands her the letter, as Mildred just stares at her.

MILDRED

I'm sorry, Mrs Willoughby . . .

ANNE

Are you? Are you really?

MILDRED

Of course . . .

ANNE

Surely it's the perfect ending for you, isn't it? It's proof that they've been successful, these billboards of yours, isn't it, a dead policeman? It's quantifiable now.

MILDRED

Are you blaming this on me?

ANNE

No, I'm not blaming this on you. I just came to give you the letter. Now, my two little girls are out in the car, so I'd better not stay and chat. I'm not sure *what* we're going to do for the rest of the day. It's hard to know what to do the day your husband kills himself. It's hard to know what to do.

Anne leaves. Mildred looks out as she drives away – and sees Polly and Jane looking back at her through the rear window.

Mildred rests her head on the glass door a second, the broken 'Welcome to Missouri' rabbit on the shelf beside her, its head split in two. She opens the letter in her hand and starts reading, as dusk falls on the street outside.

WILLOUGHBY

Dear Mildred, Dead Man Willoughby here. Firstly I wanted
to apologise for dying without catching your daughter's
killer. It's a source of great pain to me, and it would break
my heart to think you thought I didn't care, cos I did care.
There are just some cases . . .

EXT. BILLBOARD ROAD — DUSK

*The billboards and surrounding landscape from various angles at
sunset; including details like the half-eaten flowers and the insects
thereon; the burnt patch of dirt; and the billboards themselves.*

WILLOUGHBY
(*voice-over*)

. . . where you never catch a break, then five years down the
line some guy hears some other guy bragging about it in a
bar room or a jail cell and the whole thing is wrapped up
through sheer stupidity. I hope that might be true for
Angela, I really do. Second, I gotta admit, Mildred, the
billboards were a great fucking idea. They were like a chess
move. And although they had absolutely nothing to do with
my dying, I'm sure that everyone in town will assume that
they did, which is why, for Willoughby's counter-move, I
decided to pay the next month's rent on 'em. I thought it'd
be funny, you having to defend 'em a whole 'nother month
after they've stuck me in the ground. The joke is on you,
Mildred, ha ha, and I hope they do not kill you. So good
luck with all that, and good luck with everything else too.
I hope and I pray that you get him.

EXT. DIXON'S ROAD — DUSK

Dixon and Momma sitting on their porch at sunset, with beers.

MOMMA
Well, do you want *me* to go down and talk to them?

DIXON
No, I don't want you to go down and talk to them. Jesus!
Somebody sending their goddam mother down to talk to

the goddam police, for Christ's sakes. (Pause.) And say
what?

MOMMA

And say to give you your job back. And to get rid of the
black guy.

DIXON

They ain't gonna listen to some guy's mother, asking them
to get rid of some black guy. Things have moved on in the
South!

MOMMA

Well, it shouldn't've! (*Pause.*) Will they give you any money
for being laid off an' all?

DIXON

I don't know what the compensation scheme is for when
you throw a guy out of a window, Mom. I guess I shoulda
looked into that beforehand. Let me google that!

MOMMA

A couple grand, maybe? You've been there three years. Not
counting the five years at the Academy. *Six* if you count the
year you were held back.

Dixon gives her a look as he pulls on his jacket.

Where ya going?

DIXON

None of your business.

MOMMA

Off to see your fancy woman?

DIXON

I don't got a fancy woman.

MOMMA

Yeah. I *know!*

He gives her another dirty look.

DIXON

You wanna watch yourself.

MOMMA

Or you'll do what?

DIXON

Blow your goddam head off.

Momma laughs loudly. Dixon gets in his car and drives off.

EXT. ROAD APPROACHING BILLBOARDS – CONTINUOUS

Mildred and Robbie, driving a road adjacent to the billboard road, the billboards not yet in sight.

ROBBIE

Oh, did you hear the news?

MILDRED

What news?

ROBBIE

That Dixon guy threw that Welby guy out his window this morning.

MILDRED

You're shitting me. Is Welby okay?

Robbie shrugs. Mildred is sick to her stomach, and just when it seems like things can't get any worse, she turns on to the billboard road and suddenly sees . . .

You're shitting me!

. . . all three of the billboards are on fire. Mildred speeds towards them.

EXT. BILLBOARD ROAD – NIGHT

We speed towards the fiery billboards; the third totally ablaze, the second half ablaze, words still legible, the first just getting going. Mildred grabs the car's extinguisher . . .

MILDRED

Go get the one from the house!

ROBBIE

Shouldn't I call the fire department?

63

MILDRED

Fuck the fire department! They probably started it!

ROBBIE

Well, don't do anything stupid!

But Mildred's already racing towards the first billboard, spraying it all over from close up. Robbie speeds off. Mildred keeps spraying like a madwoman . . .

MILDRED
(*quietly*)

Scumbags, scumbags, scumbags. Fucking scumbags.

. . . and finally gets the first billboard out, then sprints all the way to the second, starts in on that. It's harder this time – the flames already halfway up.

She gets an idea, concentrates all her efforts on the left-side post alone and, as it starts going out, she starts climbing up it, putting out the fire bit by bit as she goes.

Finally, all the left-hand post is out and, though her hands are burnt, she gets to the top of the billboard and starts walking along it, spraying down along its length.

This starts to work, flames edging back, until, tsss tsss, the extinguisher runs out of stuff. She tosses it violently at the flames and stays standing there, staring at them, as the flames slowly start to rise towards her again.

Suddenly, Robbie pulls up, jumps out of the car and starts in on the flames below her.

ROBBIE

What the hell are you doing, Mom?!

The flames start to come under control as Mildred climbs back down. Robbie has the second billboard out by the time she's down, but the distant third is still raging. Mildred starts marching off towards it . . .

MILDRED

Come on . . .

ROBBIE

Leave it, Ma. It's too late.

Mildred storms back and tries to grab the extinguisher off him, but he won't let it go. It's paining her burnt hands terribly, but she keeps trying.

Mom, leave it, please!

Pause. Mildred makes one final effort. This time Robbie lets it be taken. She strides off to the third billboard, totally engulfed in massive flame and, exhausted, collapses to her knees in front of it. Robbie heads towards her, to see if he can help..

EXT. BILLBOARD ROAD – NIGHT

Later. The fires out, the billboards smouldering. Firemen and cops idling. Mildred's hands are being treated by a medic, as Robbie looks on. Abercrombie comes over.

> ABERCROMBIE
> How are those hands?

She ignores him. The medic moves off.

Can I ask you a coupla questions?

> MILDRED
> You can ask me all the questions you want if you take me down and arrest me.

> ABERCROMBIE
> I'm not gonna arrest you, Mrs Hayes. I got nothing to arrest you for.

> MILDRED

Not yet you ain't.

She walks off towards the second billboard and the car.

> ABERCROMBIE
> (*to Robbie*)
> We ain't *all* the enemy, y'know?

INT. MILDRED'S HOUSE, HER BEDROOM – MORNING

Mildred lying awake, thinking. She slowly sits up, slips her feet into her fluffy bunny rabbit slippers at bedside, and sits there a while; worn out, angry, depressed.

> MILDRED
> (*quietly*)
> I'll crucify the motherfuckers. (*Crying.*) I'll crucify the
> motherfuckers.

She flexes her toes in her bunny slippers, and the bunny noses look like they're sniffing. It hits her how incongruous the image is in regard to what she's saying. She smiles.

Mildred's point-of-view: of rabbit slippers, noses sniffing again.

> MILDRED
> (*rabbit voice*)
> What are you gonna do to 'em, Mildred? You're gonna
> crucify 'em? (*Normal voice.*) That's right, I'm gonna crucify
> 'em. (*Rabbit voice.*) Who you gonna crucify? The
> motherfuckers? (*Normal voice.*) That's right, I'm gonna
> crucify the motherfuckers. (*Rabbit voice.*) Jeez! Well, I guess
> those motherfuckers better watch out then, huh? (*Normal
> voice.*) Fucking A!

INSIDE CAR, DRIVING BILLBOARD ROAD — DAY

Mildred and Robbie approaching the burnt-out, blackened billboards, and see Gabriella and her news crew at the second of them. They slow down to a crawl, to listen . . .

> MILDRED
> What's this shit . . .?

EXT. BILLBOARD ROAD, SECOND BILLBOARD — CONTINUOUS

Gabriella continuing, doing a little walk past the billboard for the camera, which pans with her . . .

> GABRIELLA
> . . . and as sad as the spectacle of these burned-out billboards
> might be, in light of the death of Chief Willoughby, this
> reporter for one can't help but wonder whether this finally

puts an end to the strange saga of the three billboards
outside of Eb—

Mildred calling from the car . . .

MILDRED
This don't put an end to shit, you fucking retard, this is just
the fucking *start*, so why don't you put *that* on your 'Good
Morning Missouri fucking Wake-Up Broadcast', bitch!

*Mildred drives off at speed from the open-mouthed Gabriella, who
finally gives the cameraman the sign to cut.*

EXT. DIXON'S HOUSE — DAY

*Dixon reading a comic book on the porch, beer in hand. Momma
comes out, worried.*

MOMMA
I see on the TV there was a buncha fires lit outside o' town
last night.

DIXON
Buncha fires, huh?

MOMMA
Out at those billboards.

DIXON
Yeah, well, back when I was a cop I woulda been interested
in who set those fires cos, technically, that's arson, but as
I am no longer employed by those people I don't really give
a good god damn, now do I?

*Telephone rings, they look at each other. Dixon goes into the house and
gets it.*

DIXON
The Dixon residence. Oh, hey Sarge! How you doing? You
got any news?

DESK SERGEANT
(*off screen*)
News about what?

                              DIXON
        I dunno, about my job and stuff?

INT. POLICE STATION, MAIN ROOM — CONTINUOUS

Desk Sergeant at desk, squad room busy, Abercrombie talking to other cops in background.

                        DESK SERGEANT
        No, no. What? No. Anne Willoughby just dropped in a letter
        that Bill wrote you before he died.

INT. DIXON'S HOUSE — CONTINUOUS

                              DIXON
        Oh my God! What's it say?

                        DESK SERGEANT
                          (*off screen*)
        I haven't *read it*, Dixon, it's not my letter.

                              DIXON
        Oh. Well, I'll come right down . . .

INT. POLICE STATION, MAIN ROOM — CONTINUOUS

Desk Sergeant looks at the distant Abercrombie and the cops listening to him . . .

                        DESK SERGEANT
        Well, uh . . . I don't think that'd be such a great idea, as
        things stand, Jason. Uh, you've still got your keys to the
        station house though, right?

                              DIXON
                          (*off screen*)
Yeah.

                        DESK SERGEANT
        Well, why don't you just come pick it up when everyone's
        gone home. I can leave it on your desk for ya.

                                68

INT. DIXON'S HOUSE — CONTINUOUS

DIXON

Oh. Okay.

DESK SERGEANT
(*off screen*)
Actually, yeah, then when you're done you can just leave
your keys, save us picking 'em up later.

Dixon nods, so he won't have to cry.

EXT. POLICE STATION — NIGHT

*The dark street at night. Inside the lowered blinds of the police station
there's the faint glow of a flashlight.*

INT. POLICE STATION — NIGHT

*Dixon in the dark, empty station with a flashlight, eating Doritos,
headphones on, looks at the 'Officer Jason Dixon' envelope on his
desk, beside Angela's file. He opens it.*

WILLOUGHBY
(*voice-over*)
Jason, Willoughby here. I'm dead now, sorry about that, but
there's something I wanted to say to you that I never really
said when I was alive. I think you've got the makings of
being a really good cop, Jason, and you know why?
Because, deep down, you're a decent man. I know you
don't think I think that, but I do, Dipshit.

EXT. MAIN STREET — NIGHT

*Street deserted as Mildred, with backpack, checks to see no one's
watching, then slips inside through the taped-up door of Welby's offices.*

WILLOUGHBY
(*voice-over*)
I *do* think you're too angry, though . . .

69

INT. WELBY'S OFFICE — NIGHT

Mildred at Welby's desk in his swivel chair, phone book open to 'Ebbing Police Precinct House', telephone to her ear, backpack on table, broken window looking out on the dark police station across the street.

> WILLOUGHBY
> (*voice-over*)
> . . . And I know it's all since your dad died and you had to go look after your mom and all . . .

INT. POLICE STATION, MAIN ROOM — CONTINUOUS

Telephone on Desk Sergeant's desk starts ringing, red light flashing, but as Dixon still has his headphones on he can't hear. Phone stops ringing after a while.

> WILLOUGHBY
> (*voice-over*)
> . . . but as long as you hold on to so much hate then I don't think you're ever going to become . . .

INT. WELBY'S OFFICE — CONTINUOUS

Mildred gets up and exits frame with her backpack, leaving just the table, window and the police station in shot. Sound only of four clinking bottles taken out of backpack. Mildred moves back into shot, looks at the phone again.

> WILLOUGHBY
> (*voice-over*)
> . . . what I know you wanna become . . .

INT. POLICE STATION, MAIN ROOM — CONTINUOUS

Dixon walking around the station, reading tearfully. Passes Desk Sergeant's desk, as phone starts ringing again. He still can't hear it. After five or six rings it stops.

> WILLOUGHBY
> (*voice-over*)
> . . . a detective.

INT. WELBY'S OFFICE — CONTINUOUS

Mildred looks at the phone she's just put down, thinking, rolling a cigarette lighter around in her hand, thumbing the flint but not lighting it, until . . .

MILDRED

Fuck 'em!

She lights the lighter, and we pan with her and finally see the four Molotov cocktails she's placed on the table.

She quickly picks up and lights the first, moves to the window and launches it high out across the street. It explodes below Dixon's window, setting it and the whole wall alight.

WILLOUGHBY
(*voice-over*)

Cos you know what you need to become a detective? And I know you're gonna wince when I say this . . .

INT. POLICE STATION — CONTINUOUS

Dixon hasn't noticed the sound or the flames. He turns the letter to the second page.

WILLOUGHBY
(*voice-over*)

. . . but what you need to become a detective . . . is Love.

Dixon winces.

Because through Love comes Calm, and through Calm comes Thought. And you need Thought to detect stuff sometimes, Jason. It's kinda all you need.

INT. WELBY'S OFFICE — CONTINUOUS

Mildred tosses the second Molotov out . . .

WILLOUGHBY
(*voice-over*)

You don't even need a gun. And you definitely don't need Hate.

71

EXT. POLICE STATION — CONTINUOUS

It hits the second-storey windows, setting them alight.

> WILLOUGHBY
> (*voice-over*)
> Hate never solved nothing . . .

INT. POLICE STATION — CONTINUOUS

Dixon is wrapped up in the letter, chewing his fingernails, flames leaping behind him . . .

> WILLOUGHBY
> (*voice-over*)
> . . . but *Calm* did. And *Thought* did. Try it. Try it just for a change. No one'll think you're gay.

INT. WELBY'S OFFICE — CONTINUOUS

Mildred tosses the third Molotov out . . .

INT. POLICE STATION — CONTINUOUS

Third Molotov hits the police station door, setting it alight.

> WILLOUGHBY
> (*voice-over*)
> And if they do, arrest 'em for homophobia! Won't they be surprised!

INT. POLICE STATION — CONTINUOUS

Flames still leap outside Dixon's window as Dixon, his back to it, keeps reading.

> WILLOUGHBY
> (*voice-over*)
> Good luck to you, Jason. You're a decent man, and yeah you've had a run of bad luck . . .

INT. WELBY'S OFFICE — CONTINUOUS

In slow-mo, Mildred tosses out the final Molotov . . .

> WILLOUGHBY
> (*voice-over*)
> . . . but things are gonna change for you . . .

EXT. MAIN STREET — CONTINUOUS

In slow-mo, the Molotov arcs up across the street . . .

> WILLOUGHBY
> (*voice-over*)

I can feel it.

. . . and in normal speed, smashes in through Dixon's window.

INT. POLICE STATION — CONTINUOUS

Dixon finally notices this one, as it explodes behind him and knocks him off his feet, his desk and that whole side of the room set ablaze. He sees that the station door is on fire also, blocking his exit, and the Angela Hayes file on his desk on fire too.

He grabs and pats it against himself, getting the flames out but getting the gasoline all over himself in the process.

Dixon looks around, checks a locked back door, and realises there is no way out of the building other than through the fiery broken window.

> DIXON

Calm. Calm.

Standing in front of the window, he looks down at the file, places it safely up inside his shirt, hugs it tightly to his chest, takes a few steps back, then makes a running leap, head first through the flames and out the window.

EXT. MAIN STREET — CONTINUOUS

Dixon lands on the sidewalk in a heap, his clothes all alight. He quickly pulls the case file out from under his shirt and tosses it as far away from the flames as he can.

It lands in a clean spot, no flames touching it, which can't be said for Dixon. He rolls around, trying to put himself out, but it's just making it worse, he's like a fireball . . .

Across the street, Mildred comes out of Welby's building and sees him, horrified, just as James turns a far corner and sees Dixon on fire and Mildred in the doorway.

He sprints over and beats out the flames with his hands and clothes but Dixon's head, hands and body are badly charred. Mildred turns away from him, horrified, and sees the case file lying there, and realises what Dixon has done, as the sirens and blue lights of the ambulance and firemen arrive.

EXT. MAIN STREET — DAWN

Later. Fire almost out, building ravaged. Mildred sits exhausted on the sidewalk outside Welby's, James beside her, looking at her suspiciously. She looks away. Abercrombie comes over.

> ABERCROMBIE
> (*to Mildred*)

So what did you see?

> JAMES

Well, when we turned the corner from Spring, the fire was already raging, so, and then two seconds later the cop guy just jumps out the window . . .

> ABERCROMBIE

Wait, the *two* of you turned the corner from Spring? Where were you before this?

> JAMES

Round at my place.

> ABERCROMBIE

You two are boyfriend and girlfriend?

> JAMES

Well, it's early stages, y'know.

ABERCROMBIE
(*to Mildred*)

That right?

MILDRED

We've had a couple dates.

Abercrombie moves off, suspicious.

JAMES

So you wanna go out to dinner next week?

MILDRED

I'll go out to dinner with ya. But I ain't gonna fuck ya.

She heads off.

JAMES

Well, I ain't gonna fuck *you* neither. (*Quietly.*) I guess.

INT. HOSPITAL ROOM — DAY

Welby reading. A man, face and body bandaged (it's Dixon, though Welby can't see this) is wheeled in by a Nurse.

NURSE
(*to Welby*)

Burn victim. He's pretty heavily sedated.

Nurse leaves. Welby hobbles over to take a look. Half Dixon's hair is gone and only his eyes are visible through the bandages.

RED

Hey, man? You doing okay? Jeez, you got burned up pretty bad. You'll be okay though, don't worry. You want a glass of orange juice? I got a straw somewheres . . .

The eyes behind the bandages start to cry.

Hey, man, don't cry. You'll be okay.

DIXON

I'm sorry, Welby.

RED
(*pause*)

You know me?

DIXON

I'm sorry.

RED

Sorry for what, man?

DIXON

For throwing you out the window.

Welby realises finally, starts backing away.

RED

Save it.

DIXON

I'm sorry, man.

RED

I don't care. And stop crying. The salt'll just fuck up your wounds.

DIXON

I thought salt was supposed to be good for wounds.

RED

Well what am I, a fucking doctor?!

Welby goes back to his bed. Sound of Dixon still crying.

Dixon's point-of-view: through bandages, of the ceiling, him crying still. Then the sound of liquid pouring. Then the sound of shuffling steps. Then the point-of-view catches Welby, limping over. Carrying a glass of orange juice. He places it beside Dixon's bed and puts a straw in it.

Point-of-view follows Welby a little way back to his bed then drifts to the ceiling and remains there. As his crying continues.

INT. MILDRED'S HOUSE – CONTINUOUS

A knock on the front door. Mildred looks out through the spyhole, doesn't recognise Jerome, who knocks again.

MILDRED

Who is it?

JEROME

Oh, you don't know me really.

MILDRED

Well, what you want?

JEROME

I come about the billboards.

MILDRED

What about 'em?

JEROME

They got burned up.

MILDRED

I know that.

JEROME

I'm one of the guys who put 'em up in the first place.

Mildred opens door, vaguely recognises Jerome.

Jerome.

They shake hands.

MILDRED

What can I do for ya, Jerome?

JEROME

Well, y'know, when you're putting up a buncha posters like that, just in case any of 'em gets screwed up or torn, they give ya a set of duplicates, y'know?

Jerome shows her what he's brought up. Through the crack in the door she sees two big card rolls full of posters.

MILDRED
(*smiling*)

No, I didn't know that.

EXT. BILLBOARD ROAD, SECOND BILLBOARD — DAY

Later that day. Mildred and Robbie sloshing up the posters on the AND
STILL NO ARRESTS *billboard, as, distantly, Jerome is finishing up
with the first billboard. James is holding Mildred's ladder steady,
looking up at her.*

> MILDRED
>
> Ladder's pretty steady as it is, there, James.

> JAMES
>
> Oh, I don't mind. I like holding ladders. It takes me out of
> myself.

Mildred sighs. A car pulls up. Out gets Denise.

> DENISE
>
> Need a hand?

Squealing, Mildred gets down, gives her a hug.

> MILDRED
>
> When'd you get out?

> DENISE
>
> Hour ago. Judge threw it out, said the arrest report weren't
> filled out right. Say, you didn't burn down the police
> station, did ya?

> MILDRED
>
> No . . .

> JAMES
>
> No. She was with me the whole night.

Denise looks at Mildred.

> MILDRED
> (*shakes head, mouthing*)
>
> It's a long story.

*Jerome comes up, having finished the first billboard. Denise eyes him
up, thinks he's cute, it's mutual, and they exchange a 'Hi'. Jerome
holds up a part of the Willoughby poster.*

                    JEROME

You sure you still wanna put up the Willoughby one, him
dead an' all?

                    MILDRED

Why not? He paid for it.

EXT. BILLBOARD ROAD — DUSK

*Some weeks later. A grey and windy evening. The posters all up
beautifully, though the burnt billboards look like they could crumble
any second.*

INT. BAR — NIGHT

*Dixon slouched low in a booth, morose, bandages gone, but his burns
still visible. In a distant corner, Jerome and Denise chat quietly.*

*A truck pulls up outside. The Crop-Haired Guy and a male Pal enter,
order a couple of beers from Tony and sit in the booth behind Dixon,
not noticing him.*

INT. RESTAURANT — NIGHT

*Mildred and James at dinner at a nice restaurant, Waiter pouring
wine. Charlie and Penelope enter and pass, Charlie smiling at the sight
of Mildred with a dwarf. Mildred has a fleeting look of embarrassment,
which James registers.*

                    JAMES

Who's that?

                    MILDRED

My ex-husband. And his nineteen-year-old girlfriend.

                    JAMES

You wanna leave?

                    MILDRED

No, no. A deal's a deal.

Mildred smiles. James only partly reciprocates.

INT. BAR — NIGHT

Murmured conversation behind Dixon as he peels the label off his beer.

> CROP-HAIRED GUY
> (*off screen*)
> It was fucking wild, man, I think I was certifiably fucking insane for a while back there.

> PAL
> (*off screen*)
> When was this?

> CROP-HAIRED GUY
> (*off screen*)
> 'Bout nine, ten months ago.

> PAL
> (*off screen*)
> Were you on your own or what?

Dixon is barely listening, as Denise is staring hatefully at him from across the bar. He ignores her, slugs some beer, as the conversation behind him continues.

> CROP-HAIRED GUY
> (*off screen*)
> No, had a coupla buddies with me.

> PAL
> (*off screen*)
> Oh yeah?

> CROP-HAIRED GUY
> (*off screen*)
> Yeah.

> PAL
> (*off screen*)
> They fuck her too?

> CROP-HAIRED GUY
> (*off screen*)
> I think they got their kicks just watching, you know.

PAL
(*off screen*)

Was she hot?

CROP-HAIRED GUY
(*off screen*)

After the gasoline kicked in she was hot.

Dixon's listening now. He gets up and ambles past their booth, to get an idea of who's talking, but they clam up as they notice him passing.

EXT. BAR — CONTINUOUS

Dixon continues on out of the bar, lights a cigarette in trembling hands, takes out a pen, and makes a note of the truck's Idaho licence plate. Finishes the cigarette, goes back inside.

INT. BAR — CONTINUOUS

Dixon ambles past their booth again, coming in on . . .

CROP-HAIRED GUY

I ain't going down for that shit, last fucking day down there . . .

Guy shuts up again as Dixon sits back in his booth.

(*Quietly.*) He been there the whole time?

PAL

Who?

CROP-HAIRED GUY

Burnt-face-Jake. Keeps fucking walking up and down.

PAL

I don't know. I don't think so.

Guy goes to the bar and turns to get a good look at Dixon, who just stares at his beer. Guy gets two more beers and returns to his own booth, staring at him the whole way. Dixon gets up, ambles to the bar, glancing at the Guy as he goes.

Can I help you with something, man? You've been looking
over here all fucking night, now, unless you got something
to say to me, why don't you take your burnt fucking face
and get the fuck outta here, okay?

*Pause. Dixon goes over and sits in beside Pal, nudging him over, facing
the Guy.*

What the fuck are you doing?!

DIXON
Wait, wait, wait, wait, wait . . .

*Dixon holds his hands up, back and front, so the Guy can see there's
nothing in them, and that he means no harm.*

Just trust me, okay?

*Dixon reaches out with his empty right hand, slowly puts it behind
Guy's right ear, Guy flinching slightly, exchanging a glance with Pal.*

Just trust me . . .

CROP-HAIRED GUY
Just do the fucking trick.

*Dixon smiles, then quickly and deeply rakes his long fingernails down
the Guy's cheek, leaving a couple of deep bloody lines there.*

*Guy and Pal spring at Dixon, pummelling him horrifically, reopening
all his wounds.*

*Dixon doesn't fight back at all, in fact he just clutches his fists to his
chest to protect them. The two keep going and going, stamping on him
sickeningly. Jerome stands up . . .*

JEROME
Hey! That's enough now!

Guy approaches, menacingly . . .

CROP-HAIRED GUY
What's it to ya, fucker?

JEROME
The guy's a cop, man! He's a cop!

CROP-HAIRED GUY

Oh yeah? He ain't wearing no badge.

DIXON

(through blood)

I lost my badge. I can't remember where I lost it.

CROP-HAIRED GUY

You started this, man! I didn't do shit to you.

DIXON

I know I started it. I scratched you up like a bitch.

CROP-HAIRED GUY

That's exactly fucking right . . .

Guy kicks Dixon viciously in the head and exits with Pal, leaving
Dixon lying there. Unmoving.

INT. RESTAURANT — NIGHT

Mildred and James finishing their starters.

JAMES

Gotta use the little boys' room.

James goes off to the toilet. Charlie comes over, leaving Penelope
hanging, sits in James' seat, smiling.

MILDRED

You got something to say to me?

CHARLIE

If I'd known, we coulda double-dated.

MILDRED

Doesn't shitgirl have a curfew weeknights?

CHARLIE

No, no, in fact I was actually gonna take her to the circus
later, but there's no need now. Does he juggle?

MILDRED

I'm having one dinner with the guy cos he did me a favour,
okay?

CHARLIE

You don't have to explain yourself to me cos you're having dinner with a midget, Mildred.

MILDRED

I'm not explaining myself to you.

CHARLIE

You *kinda* are.

Across the room, Penelope makes a gesture about being left alone, as James comes back, sees Charlie in his seat.

Listen, I didn't come over to break your balls, you can date as many midgets as you want. No, I came over to say I was sorry, actually.

MILDRED

Sorry for what?

James gets back on to his chair as Charlie gets out of it.

CHARLIE

I'm sorry about what happened to your billboards an' all.

MILDRED

Yeah well, that's all water under the bridge now, I guess.

CHARLIE

Good. I'm glad. I was pretty drunk, but it still don't excuse it.

Mildred just stares at him.

All this anger, man, Penelope said to me the other day, it just begets greater anger, y'know? And it's true.

JAMES

Penelope said 'begets'?

CHARLIE

Yeah, 'It begets greater anger'. (*To James.*) Well, you take care of this little lady, okay sport? *Big* lady, compared to you, right?

Charlie returns to his table. Silence between James and Mildred a while.

84

JAMES

You alright?

MILDRED

I think I'd like to go home now.

James just stares at her.

Aw, don't gimme any shit, James? We can do this another
time, alright?

JAMES

Why would I wanna do this another time? You've been
embarrassed to be here ever since we arrived.

MILDRED

Oh, for Christ's sakes, James. *I* didn't force *you* to come on
this date, alright? *You* forced *me*.

JAMES

Forced you? I *asked* you on a *date*. Wow! Well, y'know, I
know I ain't much of a catch, okay? I know I'm a dwarf
who sells used cars and has a drinking problem, I know
that. But who the hell are you, man? You're that Billboard
Lady who never ever *smiles*, who never has a good word to
say about anybody, and who, in the evening times, *sets
fucking fire to police stations*! And *I'm* the one who's not a
catch?!

James climbs down off his chair . . .

MILDRED

James . . .

JAMES

I didn't *have to* come and hold your ladder!

*James leaves in tears, leaving Mildred drained. She glances at Charlie.
He's smirking at the scene. Mildred picks up her wine glass, picks up
her half-empty bottle, and, holding it low at her side, slowly walks over
to him. He loses his smile.*

CHARLIE

Now don't make a scene.

She looks the two of them over, bottle still in hand.

MILDRED
(*to Penelope*)
Did you really tell him 'Anger begets greater anger'?

PENELOPE
Oh! Yes! I did! I didn't make it up myself though. I can't
claim that! No, I read it on a bookmark. (*Pause.*) Which
was in a book I was reading (*Pause.*) About polio. (*Pause.*)
Polo. No, which is the one with the horses? Polio or polo?

CHARLIE
Polo.

PENELOPE
Polo!

*Mildred looks at them a moment . . . then places the bottle on the table
for them to finish.*

MILDRED
Be nice to her, Charlie. You got that?

Charlie nods imperceptibly. Mildred leaves.

INT. DIXON'S HOUSE – NIGHT

Dixon staggers in, bloodsoaked, past his horrified momma.

MOMMA
Jason!

DIXON
Just leave me, Momma, don't look at me.

MOMMA
(*crying*)
Jason! What have they done to you?

INT. DIXON'S HOUSE, BATHROOM – CONTINUOUS

*Dixon gets to the bathroom, slams door behind him, still clutching his
right hand to his chest. He looks at himself in the cabinet mirror a
second, repulsed by what he sees.*

He opens the cabinet mirror left-handed, rifles through shelves, finds an unopened tweezer set, then finds a small clean glass vial, a blank label on it.

He sits on the bath and very slowly uses the tweezers to scrape out all the Crop-Haired Guy's blood and skin trapped underneath the fingernails of his right hand, and carefully places each amount inside the vial.

Once all five fingernails are done he caps the vial and, pen in shaky hand, writes on its label H5T371, IDAHO.

Finished, he clutches it to his chest and sinks to the floor, shaking violently, Momma calling out, banging on the door.

> MOMMA
> (*off screen*)
>
> Jason?! Jason?!

> DIXON
> I'm gonna be alright, Momma. It's all gonna be alright.

INT. MILDRED'S HOUSE – DAY

Mildred, glass of wine on couch, TV on but not really watching. Knock at the door. She goes to get it. Looks through the spyhole.

Spyhole point-of-view: convex Dixon, new scars, bandages.

EXT. MILDRED'S GARDEN – DAY

Mildred sitting on swing set, Dixon standing, a repeat of the Willoughby scene from long ago..

> DIXON
> I don't wanna get your hopes up, alright, but there's a guy, and I think he might be the guy. I got his DNA. I got a lot of it, actually. They're making the checks as we speak.

> MILDRED
> He's in jail?

> DIXON
> No, but he ain't gonna be hard to find.

MILDRED

Why do you think he's the guy?

DIXON

I heard him talking about something that he did to a girl in the middle of last year. I couldn't hear all of it, but it sounded a lot like what happened to Angela. Then he beat the crap outta me. But cos of that I got a bunch of his DNA. So I wanted to let you know sooner rather than later. I didn't want you to give up hope, y'know?

MILDRED

I've been trying not to.

DIXON

Well, all you can do is try, as my momma says. Not so much about hope as about . . . well, I didn't used to be very good at English at school, so it was more, 'All you can do is try . . . to not be so crap at English.' Cos you need English, really, if you wanna be a cop. If you wanna be anything, really. (*Pause.*) Unless you live in Mexico or something. But who wants that?

He gets up to go.

MILDRED

Hey, Dixon? (*Pause.*) Thanks.

He smiles, and she watches him drive away, out past the billboards. She sits there a while, looking at them, thinking.

INT. POLICE STATION, WILLOUGHBY'S OFFICE – DAY

In the burnt-out office, Dixon is sitting down. Abercrombie closes the office door and sits across from him.

ABERCROMBIE

You did good, Jason. You did real good. But he wasn't the guy.

DIXON
(*stunned*)

What?

ABERCROMBIE

There was no match to the DNA, no matches to any other crimes of this nature, to any crimes *at all*, in fact. And his record is clean. Maybe he was just bragging.

DIXON

He wasn't just bragging.

ABERCROMBIE

Well, that's as may be. But at the time of Angela's death he wasn't even in the country.

DIXON

Where was he?

ABERCROMBIE

But I've seen his records of entry and exit to the States, and I've spoken to his Commanding Officer. He wasn't in the country, Dixon. He ain't our guy.

DIXON

He might not be *our* guy, but he still done something shitty.

ABERCROMBIE

Not in Missouri he didn't.

DIXON

Where was he?

ABERCROMBIE

That's classified information.

DIXON

Come on, man.

ABERCROMBIE

If the guy's got a Commanding Officer, and if the guy got back to the country nine months ago, and if the country where he was is classified, which country do you think he was in? (*Pause.*) I'll give you a clue. It was sandy.

DIXON

That doesn't really narrow it down.

ABERCROMBIE

All *you* need to know is, he didn't do nothing to Angela
Hayes. So we're gonna keep looking. Alright?

Pause. Dixon takes out his badge, shows it to Abercrombie.

DIXON

I found my badge after all.

*Dixon looks at it a few seconds, then slides it across the table to
Abercrombie, and leaves.*

INT. DIXON'S HOUSE – NIGHT

*Momma asleep, open-mouthed, on couch, TV on. Dixon watches her a
while, then dials a number on the phone, which he then carries into his
mom's bedroom, sitting on her bed. We now see that he has a shotgun
in his hand.*

EXT. BILLBOARD ROAD – NIGHT

*Mildred trudging the dirt at the billboards, replacing the dead pot
plants. At the third billboard, her cellphone rings.*

MILDRED

Hello?

DIXON
(*off screen*)

It's Dixon.

MILDRED
(*off screen, pause*)

Tell me.

DIXON)
(*off screen, pause*)

He wasn't the guy.

*Mildred crumples down beside the burnt patch of ground, lets out a
long, cold breath, then picks the phone back up.*

MILDRED
(*heartbroken*)

Are you sure?

DIXON
(*off screen*)

He, um, he wasn't even in the country when it happened.
So, whatever he did, he didn't do it round here. (Pause.)
I'm sorry I got your hopes up.

MILDRED

It's alright. At least I had a day of hoping. Which is more
than I've had for a while. I'd better go.

INT. DIXON'S HOUSE, BEDROOM — CONTINUOUS

Dixon idly taps the shotgun against his lips.

DIXON

Um, there was one thing I was thinking.

MILDRED
(*off screen*)

What's that?

DIXON

Well . . . I know he isn't *your* rapist. He is a rapist, though.
I'm sure of that.

INT. BILLBOARD ROAD — CONTINUOUS

MILDRED

What are you saying?

DIXON
(*off screen*)

I got his licence plate. I know where he lives.

MILDRED

Where's he live?

DIXON
(*off screen*)

Lives in Idaho.

MILDRED

That's funny. I'm driving to Idaho in the morning.

DIXON
(*off screen*)

Want some company?

MILDRED
(*pause*)

Sure.

INT. DIXON'S HOUSE, BEDROOM — CONTINUOUS

Dixon puts the phone back in its cradle. Looks at the gun in his arms. Leaves it on his bed. He looks in on his sleeping momma.

EXT. BILLBOARD ROAD — DAWN

The billboards as the sun begins to rise on the horizon.

EXT. MILDRED'S HOUSE — DAWN

Sunrise behind the empty swing set.

INT. MILDRED'S HOUSE — DAWN

Mildred looks in on Robbie, sleeping quietly, a drawing of Angela he's done pinned on the wall above his pillow.

EXT. MILDRED'S HOUSE — DAWN

Mildred puts a thermos, sandwiches and Doritos in the car. Dixon places a shotgun wrapped in a blanket inside too. Mildred looks at it lying there. They exchange a look, get in the car and drive.

EXT. BILLBOARD ROAD — CONTINUOUS

The burnt backs of the billboards framed along the roadside, as the car heads away towards the horizon.

INT. CAR DRIVING, BILLBOARD ROAD — DAWN

As the car rolls along the road, they're both quiet, nervous. They drive in silence a while.

MILDRED

Hey, Dixon?

DIXON

Yeah?

MILDRED

I need to tell you something. (*Pause.*) It was me who burned down the police station.

DIXON

Well, who the hell else would it have been?

She smiles. They drive on in silence.

MILDRED

Dixon?

DIXON

Yep?

MILDRED

You sure about this?

DIXON

About killing this guy? (*Pause.*) Not really. You?

MILDRED
(*pause*)

Not really.

They continue on.

I guess we can decide along the way.

Dixon nods. She smiles. They drive on.